P9-DMA-980

IMAGES
of America

HAMPTON
AND
HAMPTON
BEACH

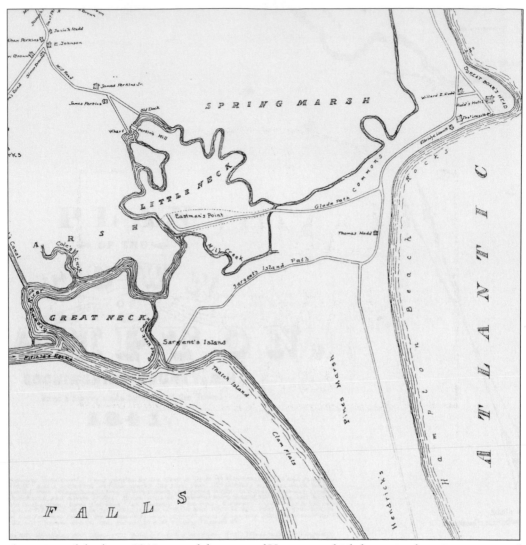

A portion of the large 1841 map of the town of Hampton which hangs in the meeting room of the town hall. Shown here is the area of Hampton Beach from Great Boar's Head south to the area of the present main beach, which at the time was a barren area called the Pines Marsh. Much of the shoreline was, even then, a fine beach. Thomas Nudd built his home at the edge of the sand in 1826, the same year his uncle David built a hotel on Great Boar's Head (see p. 64). David built another hotel nearby for his son Willard which became known as the Eagle House. Thomas Leavitt owned the Winnicumet House, the first hotel to open on Boar's Head (see p. 63). The whole area east of the river became known as the "Great Ox-Common" after a town meeting in 1641 agreed to set apart this area for the exclusive public grazing of oxen "to the world's end." That lasted only seventy-three years, although the area retained the name much longer.

IMAGES
of America

HAMPTON
AND
HAMPTON
BEACH

William H. Teschek

ARCADIA

First published 1997
Copyright © William H. Teschek, 1997

ISBN 0-7524-0440-7

Published by Arcadia Publishing,
an imprint of the Chalford Publishing Corporation
One Washington Center, Dover, New Hampshire 03820
Printed in Great Britain

Library of Congress Cataloging-in-Publication Data applied for

Selling World War II war bonds at the bandstand in front of the Hampton Beach Casino. (TM)

Contents

The dedication of Founders' Park. Horace and Elsie Batchelder unveil a plaque in honor of their ancestor at the dedication of Founders' Park. It reads: "A little band of pioneers under the leadership of Rev. Stephen Bachiler of Southampton, England seeking a larger liberty in October 1638 settled in the wilderness near this spot to plant a free church in a free town. They were joined in 1639 by others and in that year the town was incorporated. To do honor to the founders and fathers of Hampton, to exalt the ideals for which they strove and as an inspiration to posterity this memorial is dedicated October 14, 1925." (LML)

Introduction

For most of its nearly 360-year history the town of Hampton has been a small, rural community, while Hampton Beach has been frequented primarily by fishermen. Only since World War II has Hampton's population seen significant growth, accompanied by a housing boom. The Beach, on the other hand, has been a popular summer resort for more than one hundred years, attracting hundreds of thousands of people from all over northern New England and eastern Canada.

It all began in October of 1638 when a small band of pioneers led by seventy-seven-year-old Reverend Stephen Bachiler made their way up the Hampton River to found the town then known as Winnacunnet, an Indian name meaning something like "Beautiful Place of Pines." These first settlers, numbering about sixty families within the first year, laid out their homes largely in the area now bound by Park Avenue, Winnacunnet Road, and Route One. In the fall of 1639 the name was officially changed to Hampton.

Hampton originally stretched as far west as present-day Sandown. Between 1690 and 1768 nine other towns were formed from its borders, including Hampton's seacoast neighbors of North Hampton, Hampton Falls, and Seabrook, each town breaking off as its population increased and parish church became well established. In 1925 the town created Founders' Park off Park Avenue and paid tribute to its daughter towns with the erection of large stone monuments bearing the names of each of them. Smaller rock monuments were added bearing the names of the early founding families. Across the street from the park are the buildings of the Tuck Museum, created by the Meeting House Green Memorial and Historical Association. The museum holds a fine collection of old Hampton photographs, some of which were generously loaned for the production of this book.

It is unfortunate that more than two hundred years of Hampton's history could not have been captured on film. Cameras were on the scene, however, to record the rise of Hampton Beach as a popular resort. This book contains many images of hotels and other beach attractions that have long since disappeared, most of them destroyed by fire. Today's Hampton Beach bears little resemblance to the Hampton Beach of one hundred years ago.

The first hotels sprang up in the areas of Great Boar's Head in the first half of the nineteenth century. They catered primarily to fishermen or local farmers until the second half of the century, when Hampton Beach became a destination for all segments of society, from rowdy local kids to ex-Presidents of the United States. The resort flourished until the last two decades of the 1800s, when fires destroyed major hotels and competition from other area resorts led to a decline in the tourist trade.

The lack of mass transportation to and from the Beach was another factor in its decline. This situation was rectified between 1897 and 1902 with the construction of street railway lines connecting the beach and the town with Exeter, Portsmouth, Seabrook, and Salisbury. From there lines spread to the textile mill towns of Manchester, Lawrence, and Lowell, making it possible for mill workers to come here in droves. Thousands of tourists a day could travel to Hampton Beach, and in 1899 the Hampton Beach Casino was opened to attract even more. From that point on Hampton Beach's future as a popular resort was assured, and it continues unabated to this day. Even a series of destructive fires in the early part of this century couldn't dampen the enthusiasm.

The town center of the early 1900s, on the other hand, is immediately recognizable to anyone familiar with today's street front. The major changes have been in the areas of Route One north and south of the center, which have changed from the farms and residences of one hundred years ago to today's proliferation of businesses lining both sides of the road. Around the town and away from Route One Hampton remains largely residential, although the multitude of family farms have dwindled to just one.

This book is a visual tour of Hampton and Hampton Beach as they once were, fifty to one hundred years ago. It attempts to show changes in streets and buildings, particularly at the Beach, as well as glimpses of the people who lived and played here. Many of the pictures are taken from postcards, which have been produced by the thousands since quite early in this century. Others have come from private and public collections. Both the library and the town historical society are actively searching for more old photos to add to their collections. I urge anyone possessing photos of Hampton or Hampton Beach prior to, say, 1950 to contact me at the library. Arrangements will be made to have them copied.

William H. Teschek
January 1997

Hampton Beach, July 4, 1915.

One
Along Lafayette Road

The Union House, before 1890. Located at the north corner of Lafayette and Winnacunnet Roads, this hotel was built about 1816–17 by Josiah Dearborn on the site of Leavitt's Tavern, which began operation in the mid-1700s. First called Josiah Dearborn's Inn, then Samuel Dearborn's Inn (after Josiah's son), it was renamed the Railroad House in 1840 in honor of the construction of the first rail line through Hampton. In 1859 or 1860, under new ownership, it became the Union House. A large wing was added in 1886, enabling the hotel to accommodate from eighty to one hundred guests. In 1890 it was renamed the Hotel Whittier (see p. 12). (LML)

The Lafayette Road bridge over the Taylor River, near the border with Hampton Falls, c. 1896. The Hampton Causeway Turnpike Corporation was formed in 1808 to build a permanent road over the marshes to Hampton Falls. For a number of years it was a toll road, which aggravated so many travelers that a crude bridge called the "shunpike" was thrown over the river farther upstream. Despite the more circuitous route, many people preferred taking the free road over paying a toll. The towns of Hampton and Hampton Falls purchased the road and bridge from the corporation in 1826, for a price of $5,000, after which the "turnpike" became a free road. (LML)

An aerial view, looking west, of the newly created Tuck Field, Founders' Park, and Meeting House Green, c. 1930. The southern end of Lafayette Road crosses the top of the picture, forming a triangular intersection with Park Avenue and Drakeside Road. The General Jonathan Moulton House appears in the upper left. (LML)

Lafayette Road looking south from the intersection with Winnacunnet. General Jonathan Moulton's house is in the distance. In 1922, this house, one of Hampton's most historic sites, was moved 150 feet southwest from its pictured location in order to straighten out the sharp bend in Lafayette Road. Today this stretch of road is lined with a multitude of businesses, a cinema complex, and the Catholic church. (TM)

Italian workmen constructing the tracks of the Exeter, Hampton, and Amesbury Street Railway, c. 1899, along Lafayette Road near the intersection with Park Avenue. The view looks north up Lafayette Road. (LML)

Lafayette Road looking north to the intersection with Winnacunnet, and beyond, before 1890. The Union House (see p. 9) dominates the center of the picture. (LML)

The Hotel Whittier, shortly after the turn of the century. This was the area's most popular hotel and restaurant, and was the center of Hampton's social activity. Formerly the Union House, it was renamed in 1890 by owner Otis Whittier. It included a large annex on the back, a bowling alley, garage, stables, and a barn. The hotel closed its doors in December 1916, and burned down the following month. Today the site is occupied by a Shell station and a Friendly's Restaurant. (ED)

The Hotel Whittier annex, early 1900s. In 1907 the old Marston House, attached to the rear of the Hotel Whittier, was renovated for use as the town's telephone exchange. (ED)

The first Hotel Echo, adjacent to the Hotel Whittier on Winnacunnet Road. Built and owned by Charles O. Stevens, the Echo was destroyed by fire in September 1913. (ED)

The second Hotel Echo, built in 1918 on the site of the first. For the first few years this was known as the Echo House. It changed its name to the Hotel Echo by 1924, closed for a while c. 1927, and then reopened as the Whittier Inn before 1930. At right is the parsonage of the Baptist church. (ED)

The Whittier Inn. Formerly the Hotel Echo, this hotel operated from the late 1920s through the 1960s. In 1970 it became the home of Odyssey House, an adolescent drug-treatment facility which is still located at 30 Winnacunnet Road, and which houses minors who have been placed via New Hampshire's juvenile justice system. (ED)

The Toppan House, 1920s. Mary C. (Toppan) Clark operated a boarding house on the corner of Lafayette and Winnacunnet Roads. After her marriage to Lewis P. Clark in 1928 it became known as Clark's Tourist House. Mary Clark died in 1956. Before 1960 the building was moved a short distance to front on Winnacunnet Road, and around 1978, it was moved again to 35 Drakeside Road. (ED)

The Savory Street Restaurant, July 1970, at the south corner of Lafayette and Winnacunnet Roads. Formerly the Mustard Pot Restaurant, it became Savory Street when purchased by Mike and Kay Tinios. At the time it was strictly a fast-food restaurant, but it has since expanded several times and is today a full-service restaurant called The Galley Hatch. One expansion displaced the Toppan House, which can be seen in the right rear. (Courtesy Galley Hatch)

The old Toppan farm at 340 Lafayette Road. From 1837 to 1849 Edmund Toppan was Hampton's postmaster, and the town's second post office was located here. During the 1930s and '40s Christopher Toppan operated a boarding house from here. In 1971 the Olde Hampton Village apartment complex was constructed on this site. (LML)

The Edgewood Shopping Center, 350–358 Lafayette Road, about a year after its construction in 1966. The A&P supermarket operated from this location from 1967 until 1980, and was followed by the S&R Food Center. That closed c. 1987 and was replaced by a Brooks Pharmacy. The shopping center, now named Brooks Plaza, also contains four other businesses. (E&H)

A view south down Lafayette Road from the town center, early 1900s. From here the trolley tracks headed south to Winnacunnet Road, then out to the Beach or south to Massachusetts. The Odd Fellows Building is at the right. (ED)

The Odd Fellows Block when it was home to Sanborn's Drug Store and ice cream soda shop, before 1915. The automobiles were superimposed on the picture postcard to jazz it up. (ED)

A view from the railroad bridge of the train station and the Odd Fellows Building, early 1900s. The latter was built in 1895 and burned in 1990 (see p. 114). Its clock tower was added in 1898. (ED)

The Cogger Block buildings, 1923. Buck's Variety Store at the corner of Depot Yard later became the first home of Lamie's Restaurant (see next page). This block of buildings was destroyed by fire in 1943. It stood on the south corner of today's Depot Square and Lafayette Road. (TM)

Lamie's Restaurant, 1930s. Albert Lamie opened his restaurant in the Cogger Block in 1925. Before long he relocated to the old E. Warren Lane homestead on the north corner of Lafayette and Exeter Roads, where today's Lamie's Inn still operates. (LML)

The railway station, seen from the Odd Fellows Building, early 1900s. The station was built in 1900 when the Exeter Road overpass was constructed. Passenger service ended in 1965; the site has since been expanded and now contains several small businesses. The Woodbury Office Building was constructed on the north side. (ED)

The center of town, looking west down Exeter Road, before 1900. In 1900 an overpass was built over the railroad crossing seen in the picture, and it remains so to this day. Most of the buildings on the left were moved. The Joshua A. Lane store at far right is still there, where it was later attached to Lamie's Tavern. The John A. Towle house just beyond it was moved to 65 Exeter Road. (LML)

The town pump on Exeter Road, before 1900, in front of what is now Lamie's (see also p. 120). This popular horse-watering spot is being used by contractor Harry Brown (left) and Dr. Marvin Smith. The Howard G. Lane house at left was moved to 8 Dearborn Avenue when the railroad overpass was constructed in 1900. In this picture it stands approximately where the rear of Sanel Auto Parts is today. (LML)

Buildings on south side of Exeter Road, Hampton center, before 1900. The railroad crossing can be seen at right. When the overpass was built these buildings were all moved. The large Shaw Block at left was moved to 471 Lafayette Road, on the corner of High Street, and the Randolph DeLancey house to its right was moved to 294 High Street near Five Corners. (LML)

Two more businesses relocated by the railroad overpass construction, c. 1899. The John A. Towle building (right) was home to John W. Mason's dry goods store from 1875 to 1889, and the Edward B. Towle store from 1890 until the building was moved to 465 Lafayette Road, the present site of Marelli's Market. At left is the building built by Thomas N. Chase in 1883 and used by him as a store until 1890, after which it was a billiard and pool hall. It was moved to 457 Lafayette Road, later to become the Colt News Store. (LML)

Construction of the railroad overpass, 1900, looking west down Exeter Road. Some buildings have already been moved. The Chase building and pool hall at left became Colt's, and the John A. Towle home at right was moved further west to 65 Exeter Road. (LML)

The town center after the buildings were moved. The Joshua A. Lane Block, shown here shortly after it was completed in 1900, now houses Hampton Village Hardware and several other small businesses. The view looks much the same today. (ED)

Looking east down High Street, before 1900. The Cotton Brown house at left was moved east to make way for the construction of the Lane Block and is now the office of Tobey & Merrill Insurance. The shoe factory, with smokestack, was built in 1887 and can be seen in the distance (see also p. 35). (LML)

The Merrill Block, also known as the Post Office Block. Built by Dr. William T. Merrill in 1889, this block housed the post office, among other businesses, for many years. It still stands on the south side of High Street near Lafayette Road. The Shaw Block on the corner of High and Lafayette can be seen behind it, as can the railroad station water tower, which was used to supply steam engines with water for their boilers. (ED)

The traffic signal in the center of town, with the Lane Block at left, looking east on High Street. The first traffic lights in town were installed in 1924, and were replaced by new ones in 1930. (TM)

Lamie's Tavern as it looked in the 1930s or '40s. The building at left, originally the Joshua A. Lane store, has since been more fully integrated into the main building. It is occupied here by Lamie's Pastry Shoppe. Lamie's Inn is still in business today on the north corner of Lafayette and Exeter Roads. (E&H)

The Samuel D. Lane farm, 567 Lafayette Road, c. 1890. Gus Parker, a farmhand, is pictured with oxen and cart. A service station at the intersection of Rice Terrace now occupies this site. (TM)

The Work-Rite Garage, 575 Lafayette Road, after 1915. Owner Lawrence Hackett (pictured) later moved his business to the location of the following picture, where he operated a Chevrolet dealership. Several businesses have since operated on this site, but this building no longer stands. (LML)

Gale's Garage, 641 Lafayette Road. Built by Floyd and Clara Gale in 1925, they sold the business in 1944 to Lawrence Hackett, who opened Hackett Chevrolet. It is now home to the Atlantic Motor Mart and Wallace Realty, across from the entrance to Super Shop 'N Save. (LML)

The Bradford Shoe Company plant on Kershaw Avenue, late 1930s. Built by town businessmen in 1935 to bring industry to town during the Depression, the Bradford Shoe Company, owned by Clarence Kershaw of Bradford, Mass., operated here until 1949, when it was replaced by Nichols Poultry Farm. (E&H)

Nichols Poultry Farm, in the former Bradford Shoe building on Kershaw Avenue, c. 1950s. This plant was used by the Nichols chain of chicken-breeding and egg-hatching plants as a distribution center. Here the eggs were graded, sorted, and stored to await shipment to all parts of the U.S., Cuba, and Puerto Rico. In 1961 the building was bought by the Pearse Leather Company. It has since been home to numerous small businesses. (E&H)

The Deacon William Lane house, once one of the oldest houses in town. Built by Deacon William Lane around 1746, it was torn down in the 1950s and the site is now occupied by a service station at 747 Lafayette Road. At left is the home of Orrin L. Lane (the great-great-grandson of William) which was moved back to 19 Tuck Road. (ED)

Rudy's Farm Kitchen restaurant, 777–779 Lafayette Road, was in business in the 1930s and '40s. The Partridge Apartments and Garden Apartments were here later, as well as Sousa's BP station. The buildings are now gone and the lot is used for parking for the Seacoast Health Center. (TM)

Route One at the Hampton/North Hampton town line. Post Road bears off to the left, and Route One to the right. The picture was taken from the bridge over the railroad tracks. (Courtesy Michael T. Plouffe Sr.)

Two

Around the Town

An aerial view over High Street (bottom) and Winnacunnet Road (center) in the 1920s or '30s. High Street Cemetery is at lower right. Across the street and behind the Hampton Academy can be seen one of the early town dumps. The new Center School, opened in 1922, is at right center, and above and to the left of that is Tuck Field. Lafayette Road heads south in the upper right corner. (LML)

Cows in a field on the Edmund W. Toppan farm along Winnacunnet Road near the present site of the Galley Hatch Restaurant, before 1900. The Baptist church can be seen through the trees at center. (LML)

Jerome Selleck's Texaco gas station and store next to the Baptist church on Winnacunnet Road, 1940s. In the late 1800s this was the shop of tinsmith George Collum. Allison K. Chase followed Selleck with his auto sales and service business by 1949. In the 1950s and '60s it held a succession of markets including Keniston's, the I.G.A., the Hampton Food Market, and the Meat Man Market. (LML)

A view west on Winnacunnet Road, between 1910 and 1922. At left is the Congregational church, and opposite that is the old town hall and the Lane Memorial Library. Note the trolley tracks running along the left side of the road. (ED)

The Ring Swamp Cemetery on Park Avenue, c. 1896. This was the town's second cemetery, laid out in 1797, the first interment being that of Joshua Towle who died that year. The earliest existing gravestone dates from 1800, and the most recent from 1934. The home at left was built c. 1814 by John Batchelder and still stands at 60 Park Avenue. (LML)

A view west on Winnacunnet Road, in the vicinity of Park Avenue. The trolley cars are at Young's Turnout, a section of track that branched off briefly from the main line to allow two trains to pass each other. The rise of the automobile led to a steep decline in revenues for the trolley company by 1920, and in a special town meeting that December the Town of Hampton voted to purchase the trolley line. Operated primarily as a public transportation service for tourists, the line continued to lose money until finally, in 1926, it was voted during a town meeting to discontinue it, leaving a large debt to be paid. The last car ran on January 26, 1926. (ED)

Hampton's famous old elm tree. This elm spread its stately limbs over Elmwood Corner on Winnacunnet Road (at the intersection with Landing Road) from about 1773 until it was infected by Dutch Elm disease and cut down in 1959. The Elmwood Inn opened in the late 1890s and now goes by the name of The Inn at Elmwood Corners (see also p. 42). (AM)

The Jenness blacksmith shop, 284 Winnacunnet Road, *c.* 1850 to 1890s. Prior to being owned and operated by Simon L. Jenness and his son Abbott, this was the shop of Thomas Lane, born in 1785. It was located near the west corner of the intersection with Locke Road. (TM)

The Brown family homestead, 283 Winnacunnet Road, date unknown. John Brown, the first of the name in Hampton, came to town from England in 1639 and eventually settled on this site, which was occupied by his family for many generations. Smaller summer homes, one of which can be seen at left, were built behind the older family homesteads. One much older house was removed in or about the 1820s, but the one pictured still remains. (LML)

A view east on Winnacunnet Road in the vicinity of the present-day Presidential Circle and Hampton Playhouse, early 1900s. This photograph shows the residences of Richard Barker Shelton, Moses W. Brown, and L.C. Ring. The house at left is at 368 Winnacunnet Road. Brown manufactured pianos in a shop behind his home, and by 1901 the small factory was producing two pianos a week. Examples of his work can be seen in Hampton's Tuck Museum today. (ED)

Percy Jenness in a company wagon at the Samuel W. Dearborn Lumber company on High Street, opposite the end of what is now Dearborn Avenue. In 1911 the business moved across the street to the corner of Dearborn Avenue. John A. Janvrin bought the business by 1915, and he later moved it nearby to the site of the present Dearborn House at 7 Dearborn Avenue. The parents of former N.H. Governor Stephen Merrill took over the business in the 1950s. (LML)

The Charles E. Greenman Company shoe factory, c. 1920s. This building, built on the corner of High Street and Dearborn Avenue in 1887, was operated for the most part unsuccessfully by a series of shoe companies until Greenman acquired it in 1918. He operated here into the 1970s, despite a 1961 fire that gutted the fourth floor, reducing the building to its present three stories. It was renovated in 1977 and now contains several businesses. (LML)

Nelson J. Norton's blacksmith shop, 86 High Street. Norton operated the "Hampton Carriage & Smith Shop" until his death in 1926. After that his shop was run by Fred L. Blake until the mid-1930s. Prior to this Blake had a shop on Barbour Road. Pictured are George Emery (left), Nelson J. Norton (center), and Herman Brown. (TM)

Looking down Academy Avenue in the 1920s. (LML)

Windmill Hill corner, early 1900s, at the intersection of High Street and Mill Road, looking west on High Street. The name derives from the windmill built by Captain Morris Hobbs in the late 1700s. It was removed in 1852 when the "new road," now High Street, was laid out, having stood approximately where Marston Way now meets High Street. (ED)

Arthur B. Blake (1844–1931) in front of his house at 218 Mill Road, c. 1909. This is in the area of town once called "Blakeville" due to the large number of Blakes living along Mill Road near Barbour Road. (TM)

Mace Road, looking west from Five Corners. The houses, from left to right, are the Lewis S. Lamprey (1841–1930) house at 111 Mace, the William Clements house at 107 Mace (no longer standing), the Joseph I. Lamprey (1859–1941) house at 103 Mace (since 1935 the home of Norman Towle), and the C.A. Blake house at 97 Mace (the home of Bill Durkee for many years). (TM)

The Redman Shoe Company, 101 Locke Road. Edward and William Redman of Hampton opened this shoe factory in 1910 and produced ladies' slippers here until 1935. It was one of two shoe factories in Hampton in its day, and a third—the Bradford Shoe Company—opened the year Redman closed. The factory building is no longer standing, but the house remains. (TM)

The Nilus and Nilus Brook, before 1914. "The Nilus" is now North Shore Road. The path down to the water was often used by horse-drawn wagons during hot, dry summers to wet down the wagon wheels and keep them from splitting. (ED)

The junction of Routes 111 (North Hampton Road) and 27 (Hampton Road) in Exeter, near the Exeter/Hampton town line, early 1900s. The message on the back of the postcard reads, in part: "One of the beautiful places on the trolley line to Hampton Beach. Went over this route 4 times last week." (ED)

The car barn of the trolley company (right), built in 1897 and burned in 1907. The powerhouse of the Exeter & Hampton Electric Company (left) was in use until 1927 (see also p. 127). The buildings at this location have changed since this picture was taken. They stand at the southwest corner of Timber Swamp Road and Exeter Road. Prior to 1939 they were converted into a community hall, basketball court, and skating rink. After that it was the home of the American Legion until 1962. It has held a variety of businesses since then. (LML)

The Batchelder Ice House and Pond, Towle Farm Road, 1950s. Brothers Oscar and Horace Batchelder operated an ice cutting and supply business here after making this small ice pond out of what was once a tiny stream. The building is no longer standing and the site is now a park. (LML)

The first tollbooths on Interstate 95 in Hampton. Despite vehement opposition from local businesses fearing the bypassing of Route One, the state opened the new highway in 1950. Business along Route One did decline for a few years, but not for long. Imagine the traffic jams along Route One today had Route 95 never been built! (LML)

Three
Institutions

The Hampton Police Department, 1915. Hampton's force consisted of only four officers at this time. In the front row, from left to right are Chief Robert Tolman, police "mascot" Wendell "Buster" Ring, Edward MacFarland, Uri Lamprey, Ray Haselton, and John Clark (of Nashua). During the big carnival week in September extra officers were brought in from Keene and Nashua. The men in back are unidentified, although one is Officer Gilbo of Keene. (TM)

The Hampton Beach police and comfort station, on the sea side of Ocean Boulevard across the street from the casino, c. 1926. Built after town meeting voted $15,000 in 1921 for its construction, it operated as a police station until torn down in 1962. The current Hampton Beach station was completed in 1963 (see also p. 100). (ED)

A U.S. Mail wagon in front of the Elmwood Inn on Winnacunnet Road. Household and business-mail delivery uptown didn't begin until 1946. Until that time those who wanted to send or receive mail had to go to the post office or hand their mail to a local delivery man (see also p. 32). (LML)

The Hampton Beach Fire Station, c. 1938. Still in use today, it was built in 1924 after a fire destroyed the previous station, which had just been built. Next door are the Casino Garage and the second Hampton Inn, which was built after the fire destroyed the original building (see also p. 95). (ED)

The uptown fire station, located in the first floor of the building now wholly occupied by the Hampton District Court, September 24, 1968. The town's second fire station opened on New Year's Day 1933 and operated until the new station on Winnacunnet Road was built in 1977. Pictured at left is a water-tank truck; at right is the Maynard tank/pump truck, purchased in 1964. (AM)

The Center School, c. 1884. Built in 1873 at a cost of $4,485, it served as one of the town's grammar schools until 1921, when today's Centre School was built on the same site. This building was moved a short distance to the corner of Winnacunnet Road and Academy Avenue, where it was used as the American Legion Hall and uptown fire station, and later as the Hampton District Court (see next page). (TM)

Miss Evelyn Philbrick's second-grade class at the Centre School, September 1935. From left to right are as follows: (seated) Mary Pevear, Paula Brown, Electa Nudd, unknown, Abigail Janvrin, Kathleen Quinn, and Jacquelyn Cann; (middle row, standing) Alfred Corning, Harvey Elliot, Wilson Dennett, William Stickney, Donald Blatchford, Norman Welch, Wayne Elliot, William Cushing, Stephen Fields, Barbara Scruton, and Ethel Magrath; (back row, standing) Wallace Shaw, Paul Leary, Miss Philbrick, Donald Palmer, Arthur Little, James Purington, John Kuntz, and Samuel Hoyt. (Courtesy Sam Hoyt)

The old Center School building and the Hampton Town Hall (right) before it was destroyed by fire in March 1949 (see p. 114). The Center School building housed the American Legion Hall and uptown fire station at this time. Court in Hampton was held in the town hall before the fire, but later was moved into the Center School building above the fire station. Today the Hampton District Court occupies the entire building, and a new town hall occupies the site of the old. (LML)

The Drakeside School. This was one of several one-room schoolhouses in Hampton and was built probably in the 1800s and burned c. 1932. It stood at the intersection of Towle Farm, Drakeside, and Mary Batchelder Roads, which today would be in the middle of Route 95. (TM)

Hampton Academy, early 1900s. The academy was incorporated in 1810 as a privately endowed coeducational school on the secondary level called the "Proprietary School in Hampton," and later became the public high school. The first building burned in 1851 but was rebuilt the next year. It originally stood on Academy Green, now Meeting House Green, and in 1883 was moved to the site pictured, on Academy Avenue. (ED)

The present-day Hampton Academy Junior High School building, built next to the old academy building in 1939–40. The two stood side by side for only a few short months before the old building was sold at auction to a wrecking and salvage company and razed. (LML)

The East End School at the intersection of Locke and Winnacunnet Roads, on the site dedicated in 1963 as the East End School House Park. Built in 1873, the school closed in 1922 when the new Centre School opened. It was torn down in 1940. (TM)

Lunch at the East End Schoolhouse, c. 1927. After the town ceased using the building as a school it was used for a few years by Eva E. Mason as a restaurant and dance hall. An English tea was served from 3 to 5. Customers sat at old school desks while they ate. (Photo copied from 1927–29 *Exeter, Newmarket & N.H. Coast Directory*)

The Lane Memorial Library, July 18, 1931. The privately funded Hampton Library Association donated its collection to the town in 1881 to form the Hampton Public Library. Until 1910, when this building was built, it operated out of the town hall. Local businessman Howard G. Lane had the new library built for the town as a memorial to his father, Joshua A. Lane, who had just recently died. (AM)

The Lane Memorial Library, August 19, 1983. An addition was made to the back of the 1910 building in 1957. This addition was torn down in October 1983 to make way for the construction of the present building. (Author's collection)

The First Congregational Church of Hampton, founded in 1638 by Reverend Stephen Bachiler. That first church, or meetinghouse, was built before the settlers had finished their own houses. It was a temporary structure that stood for only two years on Meeting House Green, from which the name arose. Three more structures followed on this site until 1797, when the fifth church was erected. That building later became the town hall (see also p. 45). The present building, shown here, was built in 1844. The chapel at left, added in 1894, was built in memory of Reverend John Webster. (ED)

The Methodist church, c. 1906, on Lafayette Road. Originally built in 1848 at the corner of Ann's Lane and Lafayette Road, it was moved to its present location near the town center in 1881. The small building to its left was used by the Methodists before 1848, and was originally located in North Hampton as the Baptist meetinghouse. The Horace M. Lane home is the next building to the north. (ED)

The St. Peters-by-the-Sea Episcopal Church on Highland Avenue. Built in 1912, this was the first church on Hampton Beach. It was destroyed in the big fire of 1915. (ED)

St. Patrick's Church at Hampton Beach, opened for services in 1917. Catholics in town before the twentieth century were few and far between. Until this church was built, Hampton's Catholics met in a variety of places, including the casino during the summer and the tin shop next to the Baptist church during the winter. St. Patrick's was unheated and during winter months parishioners continued to meet elsewhere. In 1937 a heated chapel was added to St. Patrick's and served as winter quarters until 1948, when Our Lady of the Miraculous Medal was built on Lafayette Road. (ED)

The Hampton Beach Community Church. Located at the corner of D Street and Ashworth Avenue behind the casino, this church was built in 1924–25. (ED)

Hampton Beach's first sewer discharge pipe, September 9, 1908. This pipe discharged raw sewage into the ocean 300 yards from the low tide mark opposite Church Street. It was rebuilt in 1917 with two more pipes added, one at the mouth of the Hampton River and one between G and H Streets. These continued until 1934 when the unsanitary conditions in the water finally motivated the town to construct a treatment plant. (TM)

The State Bathhouse. The N.H. Forestry and Recreation Commission ran this bathhouse, which opened in 1937 on land created three years earlier in a massive dredging and land-reclamation project. The bathhouse included a refreshment counter, tennis courts, shuffleboard, and other games. It was torn down in 1986 and replaced with a new structure in 1988. (ED)

The U.S. Coast Guard Station, c. 1906. Situated on North Beach opposite the end of High Street, the station was opened in 1899 and performed life-saving and ship-rescue operations into the 1960s. The building was burned down in 1973 to make way for Bicentennial Park, which currently occupies the site. The Taybury Arms Hotel can be seen at left. (ED)

A gun drill at the station, before 1913. When rescuing sailors from sinking ships a line would be fired from the mobile cannon pictured here out to the ship. Seamen aboard the ship would then tie the line to the mast and rig up a breeches buoy which they could then use to make it to shore safely. (ED)

A Coast Guard Station lifeboat, with passengers and crew. Despite the serious responsibilities shouldered by the crew of the station, there were few rescues to perform and they spent most of their time training and practicing. These exercises became a popular tourist attraction. (Courtesy John Genthner and Arthur Moody)

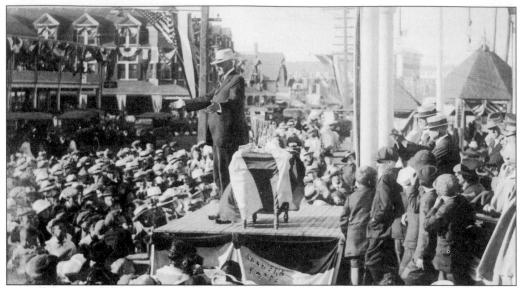

Republican Presidential candidate Charles Evans Hughes campaigning at Hampton Beach during the second annual Carnival Week in August 1916. He was unsuccessful in his bid to unseat the incumbent President Woodrow Wilson in one of the closest Presidential elections in American history. He later became the chief justice of the U.S. Supreme Court from 1930 to 1941. (TM)

Senator and Vice-Presidential nominee Richard M. Nixon campaigning at Hampton Beach, August 20, 1952. The men on Nixon's left are Hampton Judge John Perkins, U.S. Senator (formerly N.H. Governor) Styles Bridges, local businessman Ben Butler, and N.H. 1st District Congressman Chester E. Merrow. Nixon spent the next eight years in the White House with President Eisenhower. (Courtesy Louis DuBois)

Four

North Beach
and Great Boar's Head

An early pencil sketch of Great Boar's Head and the south end of North Beach. The hotel pictured is probably David Nudd's Hampton Beach Hotel, which opened to the public in 1827. Nudd opened another hotel, the Eagle House, in 1830, on the northwestern slope of the Head. It should appear here if it were in existence, so the sketch was likely made between 1827 and 1830. The Hampton Beach Hotel was later renamed the Boar's Head Hotel (see p. 64). There is a possibility that the hotel pictured is the Winnicumet House (see p. 63), which was built in 1819. It stood on the south side of the Head while Nudd's hotel was on the summit. The location in the sketch would suggest the Winnicumet House, but the building design suggests Nudd's. (LML)

The Willows, at 245 North Shore Boulevard, early 1900s. This lodging house was run by Irvin E. Leavitt and his wife Agnes for much of the first half of this century, until Irvin's death in 1942. The site is now 23 Cusack Road and is occupied by the Ocean Willows condominiums. (ED)

A view looking east toward the sea from in front of The Willows, down what is now Cusack Road. (ED)

Cusack Road from the vicinity of the fish houses. The white houses in the distance are 76 and 80 North Shore Road. (LML)

Fish houses, North Beach opposite the end of High Street, before 1911. Since at least 1809 these fishing shacks were used by local fishermen for their easy access to the sea. A long legal dispute in the 1950s led to the destruction of most of them in 1959 and the creation of a town park, which was named in honor of Ruth G. Stimson in 1965. Only two fish houses remain today. (ED)

The Leavitt Homestead and Barn Theatre at the end of High Street, with the U.S. Coast Guard Station in the lower right. This was the site of the first dwelling at the Beach, built in 1800. The Leavitt family began using it as a lodging house for fishermen in the mid-1800s, and it was later enlarged and used for tourists. The barn became a theater in 1935, and was later a restaurant and motel, before being torn down in 1988. Leavitt's is now the Windjammer Motel. (LML)

A view west up High Street from the ocean, with the Taybury Arms Hotel amidst high water, c. 1930s. To this day this area is frequently under water after bad storms. (LML)

The Taybury Arms, at the end of High Street where King's Highway enters. Opened in the early 1920s, it became the MacKenzie Arms in the 1940s, and in 1960 was renamed the Spindrift Resort Motel and extensively remodeled. The Spindrift burned in 1981 and was replaced by the Ocean Crest condominium complex. (LML)

The Leonia, a summer hotel on High Street about a half mile from the beach. The former Edmund Mason house was turned into this large hotel in 1894 which had room for sixty guests. It was destroyed by fire in July 1900 and never rebuilt. (LML)

A Grange float in front of the North Shore Hotel, 1918. This hotel stood on the north side of the junction of Winnacunnet Road and Ocean Boulevard from the early 1900s until 1971. For many years it was owned by Arthur Dumas and was called the Dumas North Shore Hotel (or the Dumas Hotel). It was replaced by a condominium complex, the Village By The Sea at 2 King's Highway. (LML)

A view south from the junction of Winnacunnet Road and Ocean Boulevard, after 1906. (LML)

The Stone Cottage at 555 Ocean Boulevard, North Beach. It was built by Mrs. Mary Aiken of Franklin, N.H., in 1894. (ED)

North Beach from Great Boar's Head, before 1920. (ED)

North Beach north of Great Boar's Head, c. 1950. A metal seawall was constructed in place of these rocks in the mid-1950s, and was in turn recently replaced by a substantial steel and concrete wall. (LML)

Great Boar's Head, 1816, from a map drawn by Philip Carragain. At left are North Beach and the fish houses. The lines on Boar's Head are stone walls, and a flock of birds flies overhead. Daniel Lamprey, who in 1806 built the farm pictured here, didn't build further up on the Head so as not to frighten the birds, which were greatly valued at the time for hunting. For a time the house doubled as a small inn run by Daniel's son Jeremiah. (LML)

Winnicumet House at Rocky Bend on Boar's Head. This was the first hotel on Boar's Head, and one of the first seaside hotels north of Boston. Built in 1819 on the southern base of the Head, it burned under suspicious circumstances in 1854 and was never rebuilt. (LML)

A painting of Hampton Beach and Great Boar's Head, possibly from the 1860s. A fish house is in the foreground and the Hampton Beach Hotel/Boar's Head Hotel appears in the middle of Boar's Head. (LML)

The Boar's Head Hotel, *c.* 1880s. This hotel, opened in 1827 by David Nudd as the Hampton Beach Hotel, was later renamed. It was purchased by Colonel Stebbins H. Dumas in 1866, and was destroyed by fire in September 1893. (LML)

Another view of the Boar's Head Hotel, with carriages full of tourists. (LML)

The Granite House Hotel, built in the mid-1800s at the northern base of Great Boar's Head. Before 1892 it was renamed The Rockingham, and in 1901 it became the New Boar's Head Hotel (see p. 68). The "old" Boar's Head Hotel can be seen at right higher on the Head. (LML)

A wide-angle view of Great Boar's Head in 1872, taken from the south. At far right is the Boar's Head Hotel; the large building in the center is the brand new Leavitt's Hampton Beach Hotel. (ED)

Leavitt's Hampton Beach Hotel, c. 1885. Built in 1872 on the site of the old Winnicumet House, at the southern base of Boar's Head known as Rocky Bend, Leavitt's was a popular Hampton Beach hotel for half a century until it was torn down in 1921. (LML)

Rocky Bend and Leavitt's Hampton Beach Hotel, looking south, probably early 1900s. (ED)

An early 1900s view of Leavitt's. In 1872, the year it opened, Presidential candidate Horace Greeley gave a campaign speech here. He lost to incumbent President Ulysses S. Grant, and then died less than a month after the election. After Leavitt's was torn down in 1921, the Dance Carnival was built on this site (see p. 69). (ED)

The New Boar's Head Hotel, opened in 1901 at the northern base of Boar's Head. This was previously the Granite House and the Rockingham Hotel. The hotel burned in 1908 and wasn't reopened. (LML)

Another view of the New Boar's Head Hotel, 1901–1907. It was opened by Colonel S.H. Dumas, the owner of the "old" Boar's Head Hotel that burned in 1893 (see p. 64). He died in 1902, however, and it continued under new management. Today's Dumas Avenue on Boar's Head is named after him. (ED)

Boar's Head from North Beach before 1908. The New Boar's Head Hotel is the large building at center. Most of the other buildings are private residences. (ED)

The Dance Carnival, shortly after it was built at Rocky Bend on the site of Leavitt's Hampton Beach Hotel in 1921. This was a popular Beach attraction until the casino built its own dance hall in 1927. The Dance Carnival declined after that and was on the verge of going out of business when it burned in November 1929. (ED)

The Rocky Bend restaurant and market, c. 1940, built on the site of the Dance Carnival after it burned in 1929. This restaurant remained a popular eating spot into the late 1970s, when it was torn down and replaced by the Rocky Bend Condominiums, one of the first of many condo complexes at the Beach. (LML)

The Boar's Head Inn, 19 Dumas Avenue. This long-standing inn was built after an early inn by the same name burned in January 1929. For a while in the 1930s it was the only hotel on the beach open year-round. It operated until 1985 and is now condominium housing. (ED)

An aerial view of Boar's Head and North Beach, 1950. The large water tower, or "standpipe," was built in 1907 to supply water to the Beach for firefighting and domestic purposes. It was also used by mariners as a landmark until taken down in 1966. (ED)

Five

South of Boar's Head to C Street

The Ocean House, built in 1844 and destroyed by fire in 1885. It was and still is the largest hotel ever to be constructed on the Beach, eventually standing four stories high with rooms for 250 guests. Not to be confused with a later Ocean House that stood next to the casino, this Ocean House was located just north of today's Church Street. When it was built it was one of the only buildings on Hampton's coast south of Boar's Head. (LML)

An early 1900s view of the northern section of Hampton Beach. The "standpipe," built in 1907, can be seen on Boar's Head in the distance. (ED)

The Merrimac House, 425 Ocean Boulevard, before 1933. Opened before 1915, it was called the Merrimack Seaside Inn from the 1970s until it closed c. 1984. It is now the site of the Coastview Condominiums. (ED)

The Seven Gables, 405 Ocean Boulevard. Opened by 1949 by real estate agent J. Walter Hollis, it had both cabins and rooms. It is still in existence today as private condominiums. (ED)

Cutler's Sea View House, 387 Ocean Boulevard. This building was built after an earlier Sea View was destroyed in the 1885 fire that also took the Ocean House. In the 1940s it became the Constance Hotel, owned by Edgar P. Lessard; in 1949 it was purchased by Mr. and Mrs. Herbert Allen of Amesbury and became the Hotel Allen. (ED)

The Hotel Allen, formerly Cutler's Sea View House and the Constance Hotel. It was later known as the Allen House and finally, for only a few months, as the Rock Harbor Inn, its last name before being destroyed by fire on October 1, 1985. Today the lot is vacant and used for parking. (ED)

The Gookin House, 379 Ocean Boulevard. Built in 1898 as an annex to Cutler's Sea View House, it was called Cutler's Cafe or Cutler's Annex until the mid-1920s. It was called the Cavalier Hotel from the 1940s until it closed c. 1986, and is now a restaurant called Ron's Landing at Rocky Bend. (ED)

The Winona at 15 Church Street, a long-standing lodging house operated by Hypolite J. Croteau and his wife Winona since the 1920s. It went out of business in the 1970s but the building still stands and is used for rental housing. (ED)

DeLancey's Hotel, located just north of the original Ashworth Hotel on land that the Ashworth has since expanded onto. It was destroyed in the big 1915 beach fire when firefighters dynamited it in a successful effort to halt the northern movement of the blaze. It was rebuilt in 1921 and stayed in business into the 1950s. (1915–17 *Exeter & NH Coast Directory*)

The original Ashworth Hotel, opened on Memorial Day in 1912. Owner George Ashworth was for many years a prominent businessman, civic leader, and precinct commissioner. Marsh Avenue was renamed in his honor in 1957. This first Ashworth Hotel was destroyed by fire in November 1913 after only two seasons in business. (ED)

The second Ashworth. Built on the ashes of the first, this building had an equally short life, and burned to the ground in the big beach fire of 1915. DeLancey's Hotel can be seen at right. (ED)

The third and final Ashworth, built in 1916. A testament to the perseverance of owner George Ashworth, who built three hotels in five years, this building remains as one of the most prominent landmarks at the Beach. (ED)

Hampton Beach from the front plaza of the Ashworth, c. 1920s. (ED)

The main section of Ocean Boulevard, looking south from in front of the Ashworth, c. 1920s. (ED)

The Imperial stood near the corner of Marsh (now Ashworth) Avenue and Ocean Boulevard for only a few years before it was destroyed in the beach fire of 1921. (ED)

An early 1900s view of the beach and Ocean Boulevard from the Dudley & White store at the north corner of C Street north to Jenkins Cafe (far right). (ED)

Jenkins Cafe, at the corner of Marsh (now Ashworth) Avenue and Ocean Boulevard. This was one of the many buildings destroyed in the 1915 fire. Jenkins afterward built a hotel on the same site, but that too was destroyed by fire in 1921. (ED)

The second Hotel Radcliffe, just north of A Street and south of Jenkins Cafe. The first Radcliffe, built in 1900, burned in 1901. In 1909 the second Radcliffe, too, succumbed to fire, and was replaced by the Grand View House. (ED)

The Grand View House, built just south of Jenkins Cafe after the Radcliffe burned. This was one of the many buildings destroyed in the 1915 fire. The Olympia Theatre was built in its place. (ED)

The Olympia Theatre section of Hampton Beach, between the fires of 1915 and 1921. Two earlier Olympia Theatres in other locations had been destroyed by fire, as was this one in 1921. It was rebuilt for a third time and stayed in business into the 1950s, when it was replaced by the Surf Hotel and Theatre. (ED)

The Surf Hotel at 275 Ocean Boulevard. A number of small businesses occupied the lower levels, including the Surf Theatre and a post office. The Surf Hotel and Hudon's Restaurant are still in business today. (ED)

The Garland hotel, not long after it was built on the northern corner of A Street after the 1921 fire. The lower level was home to a Philip Morris & Co. shop and Lamb's grocery store. The Garland hotel changed its name to the Hotel Standish in the mid-1930s. (ED)

The Hotel Standish, formerly the Garland. Lamb's grocery store was still in residence on the lower level. The Standish remained in business until the 1970s. Today the Happy Hampton Arcade occupies the first floor. (ED)

The Lawrence House, 7 A Street. Mrs. Katie M. Harrington started a small rooming house with only six room on this lot in 1901. It was destroyed in the 1915 fire and was rebuilt with twenty-three rooms, as pictured here. It burned again in the fire of 1921 and was rebuilt with thirty-seven rooms and a large dining room. It was renamed the Hollingworth Hotel in the mid-1950s. (ED)

The Antler hotel on A Street, on the south side of the street two doors up from Marsh (now Ashworth) Avenue. Mrs. Lillian G. Cotes from Cambridge opened the hotel in 1921, and advertised it in the local business directory as being Hampton Beach's newest hotel. Unfortunately, by the time the directory was printed, the hotel had been completely destroyed in the June 1921 fire. It was never rebuilt. (ED)

The first Janvrin Hotel, before 1910. In 1911 it was purchased by Mrs. Florence Munsey, who moved this building behind Jenkins' Cafe at the corner of Ocean Boulevard and Marsh (now Ashworth) Avenue. She then built a new Janvrin on the site of the old. (ED)

The second Janvrin Hotel, shortly after it opened in 1912. Located at the site of the old Janvrin on Ocean Boulevard and the south side of A Street, it was destroyed in the big September 1915 fire, as were all of the buildings in this image. The Fairview Hotel is at far left. (ED)

The third Janvrin. Still owned by Mrs. Munsey, this hotel was built after the 1915 fire and destroyed in the 1921 fire. (ED)

The fourth and final Janvrin Hotel, built after the 1921 fire. Munsey's Sea Grill Restaurant was inside. In the spring of 1937 new owner William Clancy sold the hotel to longtime employee Ralph Moulton. The hotel was thereafter called the Moulton/Janvrin, and later, just the Moulton Hotel. Ralph Moulton was also the owner of the Ashworth Hotel from 1944 to 1952. (ED)

Ocean Boulevard, *c.* 1906, looking north from B Street, with the Fairview Hotel at left. (ED)

The Fairview Hotel, *c.* 1911, on the northern corner of B Street at Ocean Boulevard. The Janvrin is two doors to the right. (ED)

A remodeled Fairview Hotel, 1915. The new Strand Hotel and Theatre was built in 1915 between the Fairview and the second Janvrin (at right). All of these buildings were destroyed in the September 1915 fire (see p. 112). (LML)

The new Fairview, not long after it was built from the ashes of the 1915 fire, in a view down B Street. The Fairview Pharmacy was on the lower level. This building was destroyed in the 1921 fire. (ED)

Ocean Boulevard from the last Fairview, built after the 1921 fire, looking north to the DeLancey (at far right). In the 1960s the Fairview became the Ebb Tide Hotel, and later was the site of Jeremiah's Dance Club. (Courtesy Claire Bourque)

Portsmouth Avenue, now B Street, c. 1911. At right is the first Fairview Hotel. The Wigwam and the Avon Hotels are on the south side of the street at left. (ED)

B Street hotels the Wigwam, the Avon, and the Belle Villa, c. 1910. The Wigwam, at 7 B Street, was later owned by Dennis J. "Dan" Mahoney, a barber who moved his shop from Haverhill to Hampton Beach in 1914. The Wigwam went out of business after 1966 and the building lot is now used for parking. (ED)

The Avon Hotel, 15 B Street, before 1920. This hotel was built in 1900 by George Ashworth and operated by him until 1913, when it was purchased by Thomas and Ethel Powers. Several additions had been made to the hotel by the time of this picture. In 1939 it was bought by John W. Dignon. It was seriously damaged in the beach fire of 1950, but stayed in business until 1987. It was torn down in 1989 and replaced by a parking lot. (ED)

The Belle Villa, 19 B Street, c. 1905. The Belle Villa was built in 1903 by Edwin Janvrin and was in business into the 1940s. After that it was called the Edgewood Inn into the 1970s. The building is now used for rental housing. (ED)

The Dudley & White store, photo studio, and cafe, c. 1914. This store was established in 1895 at the north corner of C Street and Ocean Boulevard. The swastika symbol on their sign was at the time an ancient symbol of good luck, until it was forever corrupted by the Nazis. Dudley's clothing store still occupies this site today. (ED)

A 1950s or 1960s view of Ocean Boulevard from Dudley's at the corner of C Street, to the Playland Arcade and beyond. The original Dudley's and Playland (which opened in the 1930s) were both destroyed in the 1950 beach fire. (ED)

The Hill House and Hill's Cafe on Adventure Avenue, now C Street, c. 1908. These businesses lasted into the 1930s. (ED)

The Malcolm, 20 C Street. Mr. and Mrs. Wilbert J. Miller first opened it as the cottage "New Hampshire" in 1912. It was later renamed the Malcolm and stayed in business into the 1970s. The Longview Apartments now occupy the site. The Millers opened the Wilbert Hotel next door in 1915. (ED)

The Colony Cabins
Marsh Ave. at C St.
Hampton Beach, N. H.

The Colony Cabins on Marsh (now Ashworth) Avenue opposite the end of C Street, with a view west across the marsh. Opened by 1938, it later became the Colony Motel, which is still in business at 46 Ashworth Avenue. (ED)

Six

Around the Casino

The Casino, Opera House, and Ocean House, c. 1905. This wide-angle, distorted view of the Beach's most popular attraction shows the walkway over D Street that connected the Ocean House (right) to the Casino. When the Casino was built in 1899 it was almost alone among a sea of sand dunes in the unused southern section of the beach. The center of Hampton Beach activity up to this point was in the area of Boar's Head. The Ocean House followed in 1900, and the Opera House in 1901, leading a building boom that moved the center of activity to where it is today. (ED)

The Ocean House, early 1900s. Named for the Hampton Beach hotel that burned in 1885, this fifty-seven-room hotel was built by Wallace D. Lovell in 1900 just north of D Street and the Casino. At left is a view down D Street with the Hampton Inn in the distance. (ED)

The Ocean House, decked out for Carnival Week, 1915. The building was torn down in 1976 and replaced with a McDonald's Restaurant. Several small fast-food businesses also occupy the site today. (ED)

94

A view down D Street to the Hampton Inn, before 1924. (ED)

The Hampton Inn on Marsh (now Ashworth) Avenue, at the foot of D Street. Built by Casino owner Wallace Lovell *c.* 1901, it was destroyed by fire in 1923, but was rebuilt on the same site. In the 1950s it became the Janmere Motel, which it remains to this day (see also p. 43). (ED)

The Hampton Beach Casino, early 1900s. Before it was even two years old this new attraction drew thousands of vacationers to this long, wide, sandy stretch of beach that heretofore hadn't been as accessible. Nearly one hundred years later the Casino is still thriving. (ED)

The Casino contained a convention hall, restaurant, dining hall, theatre, bowling alley, billiards, and a dance hall. Daily band concerts were held at the newly constructed bandstand across the street, and fireworks were held every week. Behind the Casino was a baseball field (see p. 120). (ED)

The soda fountain and gift shop at the Casino, c. 1929. (ED)

Trolley cars arrive at the Casino. As soon as the Casino was built the streetcar company extended the trolley lines to reach it. The bandstand (left) and the Opera House (on the left side of the Casino) were built in 1901. Notice the empty sand dunes to the south of the Casino complex. (ED)

A bird's-eye view from the Casino looking south, early 1900s. The bandstand stood opposite the southern end of the Casino. (ED)

The boardwalk, built in 1911, shown here in front of the Casino and the Ocean House. Note the refreshment stand at center before the bandstand. (ED)

A popcorn and refreshment stand on the boardwalk, c. 1914. This stand was probably owned by the street railway, whose ticket booth can be seen just to the left of the stand. The railway company paid the town $100 for a license to sell popcorn here, while Robert B. Ring paid $300 for a more lucrative location right on the beach, but only a few yards away. (LML)

The Hampton Beach Chamber of Commerce (the tall building at left), opened before 1927. All of these buildings, including the bandstand, were replaced by today's Sea Shell, which was built in 1962. (ED)

The police and comfort station (at center), built in 1921. The area between the station and the bandstand was used for concert seating and other entertainment activities. The small building on the beach at left is R.B. Ring's popcorn stand (see also p. 118). (ED)

The rise of the automobile. The area south of the police and comfort station was used as a parking lot, much as it is today. In the comfort station, users were required to put a coin in a slot to gain access to a stall. A fair amount of revenue was generated this way. (ED)

Seven

The South End
of the Beach

The "Mile Bridge" over the Hampton River connecting Hampton and Seabrook beaches. Casino owner and beach developer Wallace Lovell and the trolley company began construction of this bridge in May 1901, and it opened to the public a year later, just in time for the summer season at the beach. The 4,923-foot bridge, being just 350 feet short of a mile, was the longest wooden structure of its type in New England, if not the world. It was located just west of the present bridge, which replaced this one in 1949 (see also p. 110). (ED)

Ye Colonial Inn, on the south corner of Ocean Boulevard and F Street, c. 1920s. Opened in the mid-1920s, this hotel is still in business at the same location today. (ED)

The Tides Hotel, in a view up Ocean Boulevard, c. 1950. Opened by Kenneth W. Langley after World War II, this hotel stood on the north corner of G Street. Its square architecture was considered ugly by many. The Tides was destroyed by fire in October 1974 and was never rebuilt. (ED)

The Pelham Hotel, c. 1906. This hotel was built c. 1902 on the south corner of G Street, one of the first to be built south of the Casino. A sixteen-room addition was added to the back in 1911, and it has continued to grow ever since as it remains in business to the present day. (ED)

The Hill Crest, c. 1908. This hotel was built in 1902 for William W. Ham of Haverhill on the south corner of H Street. With three stories (and a basement), forty rooms, and a first-class restaurant, it was one of the finest hotels on the beach at the time of its construction. It is still in business today as the Hillcrest Motor Inn, and is also home to Mama Leone's Restaurant. The Puritan (at left) is also still there. (ED)

The Marilyn, 17 I Street, c. 1920s. Built in 1920 by Albert Moody, the grandfather of Hampton Selectman Arthur Moody, and run by Albert's daughter, Anna Arnfield, the Marilyn was later greatly expanded and a sister hotel, the Montreal, opened next door. Neither hotel is in business today. (ED)

The Pentucket hotel. First built on the south corner of I Street and Ocean Boulevard, the Pentucket was destroyed by fire in November 1911, along with five nearby cottages. A rebuilt, four-story Pentucket, perhaps the one pictured here, burned only a few short months later in May 1912. (ED)

The New Pentucket. Built from the ashes of its two predecessors, this building remained standing until destroyed by fire again in 1961. In the 1930s its named was changed to the Beach View, which is still in business at this location. (ED)

The Lincoln House at 95 Ocean Boulevard. Opened c. 1930, it stayed in business until 1991. McGuirk's Ocean View restaurant, pub, and hotel now occupies this site. (ED)

The Springfield at 89 Ocean Boulevard between K and J Streets. Opened in the 1930s, it is still in business today as the Springfield Motor Lodge. It was first owned and operated by William B. Sears of Chicopee Falls, Massachusetts. (ED)

The Shore View, at 75 Ocean Boulevard and the north corner of L Street. Opened before 1915, the building was moved c. 1958 to 180 Ashworth Avenue where it became part of Brownie's Motel. The Harris Sea Ranch Motel expanded onto the old Shore View lot. The building pictured immediately behind the Shore View was moved to 12 Q Street. (ED)

The Langford House, *c.* 1920, on the east side of Ocean Boulevard at the south corner of Concord Avenue. The Langford was in business from before 1915 into the mid-1920s. It is no longer standing and the site is now occupied by the Drift Motel at 18 Ocean Boulevard. (ED)

The White Rock House at 20 River Avenue between Concord and Dover Avenues. Opened *c.* 1917 by Armas Guyon, it was purchased by Fred Lorenz when he moved here in 1921. Both men came to own several other beach businesses. This one stayed in business into the 1970s. In addition to rooms, the White Rock House offered groceries, a dining room, and an attached garage, which did repairs and sold auto supplies. (ED)

Lorenz's Fish Market, at the southern junction of Marsh (now Ashworth) Avenue and Ocean Boulevard, c. 1920s. The fish market, which was also a gas station and grocery store, was another business owned by Fred Lorenz. His wife operated the Sea Shell restaurant next door. Here the carcass of the small whale is being used for advertising. (AM)

Sullivan's, formerly Lorenz's, c. 1949. This business was owned by a succession of individuals after Fred Lorenz, including Howard C. Page, James J. Sullivan, Wallace Robinson, and J. Robert O'Brien. It usually had a restaurant attached, and was later known as the Bridge Market. (TM)

The Smith and Gilmore Fishing Pier and lobster pound on Hampton Harbor, late 1940s. Claude Gilmore began his fishing business in 1924. His wife Helen and her father, Nelson (Roy) Smith, opened the Smith and Gilmore fishing party business in 1944, which is still in the same location. (ED)

Cottages at White Rocks Island, c. 1910. White Rocks was a section of beach in the general area of today's state park, extending out across the current harbor inlet toward the Seabrook side of the river. Formerly an island, shifting sands attached it to Hampton Beach before the turn of the century, and buildings sprang up so rapidly that it eventually became the Beach's largest cluster of summer cottages. Storms and severe erosion put it back under water between 1914 and 1928. (ED)

Fishing boats await their owners in the Hampton River on the shore of White Rocks Island, c. 1913. This area was east of the Mile Bridge and the land at right reaches towards the Seabrook side of the river. (ED)

The Mile Bridge and the Hampton River, looking west from White Rocks Island. The bridge was a toll road that made good money for its owners for many years. Eventually, in 1933, it was purchased by the state, who continued to charge tolls. The wooden planking was a great fire hazard, and small fires caused by discarded cigarettes kept local firefighters busy, often several times a day during the busy summers (see also p. 101). (ED)

Eight
Shipwrecks, Fires, and Storms

A shipwreck on the beach just south of Boar's Head, before 1885. The large building at right is the Ocean House, which burned in 1885 (see also p. 71). To its right is Cutler's Sea View. The larger buildings on the left belonged to members of the Nudd family, located just north of today's Nudd Avenue. They were some of the first buildings built south of Boar's Head. South of these were only a few crude cottages. (LML)

The wreck of the Gloucester fishing schooner *Mary A. Brown*. All hands on board drowned in the December 1900 accident, which left this wreck on the main beach, the subject of artists and photographers for a decade. (ED)

The great fire of September 23, 1915, Hampton's worst disaster. It began in a box of rubbish on B Street and quickly spread north, fanned by strong winds, eventually leveling an area a half mile long by a quarter mile wide. This picture shows the Fairview Hotel at the corner of B Street going up in flames. (ED)

The aftermath of the 1915 fire, with the remains of the Ashworth in the foreground, looking northeast toward the steeple of St. Patrick's Church. In all, forty-two buildings were destroyed, including hotels, theaters, and the St. Peter's-by-the-Sea Episcopal Church. (ED)

An aerial view of the Beach after the great fire of June 28, 1921. The Ashworth Hotel (upper left) was spared in this blaze, which destroyed almost the same area as the 1915 fire. Buildings just north of A Street are shown here being rebuilt. Just north of the Ashworth the DeLancey Hotel is finally being rebuilt after being lost in the 1915 fire. (ED)

Firefighters battling the town hall blaze in the early morning hours of March 19, 1949. The only firefighter on duty in station number two, next door to the town hall, slept through the start of the fire, giving it a 15-minute head start. The building had to be torn down, and the current town hall was erected on the same spot. (TM)

The remains of the Odd Fellows Hall in the center of town after the January 20, 1990 fire. The building was razed and the lot is still vacant. (TM)

The Casino and the Opera House at Hampton Beach during the winter of 1905. (ED)

A snow plow north of the Casino in February 1934. The chamber of commerce building can be seen at left. (LML)

Electrical lines knocked down along Route One near the Hampton Falls border. (E&H)

Storm damage in the White Rocks Island section of the beach, c. 1931. The Mile Bridge can be seen at far left. (E&H)

The aftermath of a storm. A winter storm, date unknown, nearly carried this Hampton Beach house out to sea. (E&H)

Stanwood Brown in front of a damaged White Rocks Island cottage, 1929. The old wooden breakwater in the background was largely ineffectual in protecting beach property from severe storms. (LML)

The Ring family popcorn stand on the beach after a storm, *c*. 1930 (see also p. 100). (LML)

A beached whale on the north side of Boar's Head, *c*. 1925. (LML)

Nine

At Work and at Play

Runners line up for a footrace on Ocean Boulevard, c. 1880s. Great Boar's Head and Leavitt's can be seen in the background. Such races were a common occurrence at Hampton Beach festivals, although the number of participants was small by today's standards. (LML)

Two young girls at the town pump in the center of town, before 1900. The pump, built in 1886, was located on Exeter Road in front of what is now Lamie's Inn (see also p. 20). This photograph was taken by Mary (Toppan) Clark, who captured many images around town before the turn of the century. (LML)

A baseball game behind the Casino, *c.* 1908. (ED)

The Hampton Fishing Clique, 1909. From left to right are Charles Harrison (a blacksmith from Hampton Falls), Eugene Janvrin (a meatman), and at the far right is Walter Goss (a local house painter). (LML)

The Indian Camp at Hampton Beach, early 1900s. As early as 1861 Indians put up a tent at the beach where they told fortunes and sold baskets they made out of marsh sweet grass. In August 1911 the newspaper reported that they were camped on the site of the burned Radcliffe Hotel, led by an old squaw named Mollawantan. At the time it was one of the most popular attractions on the beach. (ED)

Dressed-up tourists in front of the Casino during Carnival Week, *c.* 1915. (ED)

Beach-goers on the sand in front of the Casino, Opera House, and bandstand. Notice the old wooden seawall. (ED)

Children on the raft at Hampton Beach. Great Boar's Head and the "standpipe" can be seen in the background. (ED)

Stunt flier Charlie Sonier parachuting onto Hampton Beach during Carnival Week, 1916, while a crowd of thousands looks on. He landed near I Street, injuring his side slightly. Pilot Farnum Fish entertained crowds during Carnival Week with passenger rides and demonstrations of aerial warfare. Carnival Queen Clara Dudley was given a long ride to the south end of the beach and back. (ED)

An airplane on Hampton Beach, *c.* 1920. Stunt flying and airplane rides were a frequent attraction at Hampton Beach during the first years of this century, beginning with the first Carnival Week in 1915. (LML)

The first beach bandstand, built across from the Casino in 1900. This photograph was taken after 1916, when the bandstand was lowered to the level of the boardwalk and the canopy was added to improve the acoustics. (ED)

The bandstand, c. 1950s. Speakers were added to the roof of the bandstand by 1936. In 1963 it was replaced by today's Sea Shell building. (ED)

George Kershaw, Herman Brunn, and Dan Scully on a break from their labors for the Exeter & Hampton Electric Company, 1924. The Methuen Hotel at the corner of H Street and Ocean Boulevard is in the background. (E&H)

Fred Perkins and his team of horses "Prince" and "Bertha" pulling a large load of hay, August 1924. His farm was along Landing Road. (LML)

The 1925 "Queen of Hampton Beach" and her "King"—Charlotte Bristol and Billy Robinson—on I Street in front of the Marilyn Hotel. Mae McCarthy (top right) and a woman named Margie hold a hotel sign above the car. (AM)

Fred Marston working in the Exeter & Hampton Electric Company's substation on Exeter Road, in the building adjacent to the old car barn, before 1928. Electrical power was produced here until 1927. (E&H)

An Exeter and Hampton Electric Company employee, dressed and ready to participate in the Hampton Beach Carnival festivities, perhaps in 1932. (E&H)

The John C. White Memorial Playground, c. 1942, located on the sands opposite A and B Streets. This children's playground was built by Precinct Commissioner John C. White in the 1920s. After his death in 1927, it was renamed and taken over by the Hampton Beach Village District. When the state built the new seawall in the 1950s it was relocated south of the Casino. It has been in its present location since 1954. (ED)

Acknowledgments

The source of each photograph is given at the end of each caption, and is usually an abbreviation, as follows: (AM) Arthur Moody, (ED) Emile Dumont, (E&H) Exeter and Hampton Electric Company, (LML) the Lane Memorial Library, (TM) Tuck Museum. A few photographs came from other sources, and full credit for these are given in the captions. Special thanks go to Hampton Falls postcard collector Emile Dumont, who let me borrow his large collection for four months.

The library's large collection of old photographs was created by Peter Randall for his excellent book *Hampton, a Century of Town and Beach, 1888–1988*. They were gathered from Hampton citizens too numerous to mention here. Much of the historical information used in the preparation of this photographic history was gleaned from Randall's book.

Hampton's Tuck Museum generously made loan of some of its excellent collection of historical photographs for this project. There are many more photos in their collection that are yet unpublished, and are worth a visit.

Thanks also to local historians Helen Hobbs, Arthur Moody, and Ansell and Irene Palmer for proofreading the manuscript in search of errors.